KU-169-075

This is Sally and her sister Kate, with their mum and dad. Sally is three years younger than Kate.

Brian's sister is much older than him. Sometimes she helps their mum look after him.

meet the family
my Sister

by Mary Auld

W
FRANKLIN WATTS
Schools Library and Information Services
NEY

S00000711653

Briony and Louise are identical twins. Only their mum and dad can tell which sister is which.

Anne has a new baby sister, Lucy. Lucy has a different mum from Anne, so she's her half-sister.

Nicky and Ruby are best friends – and step-sisters. They have different parents, but now Ruby's dad is married to Nicky's mum.

Kevin and his sister go to the same school but are in different classes.

Mary's sister is in a football team.

Miguel's sister paints
beautiful pictures.
Sometimes she lets
Miguel help.

Lizzie teases her sister.

Gareth makes his sister giggle.

Leo and his sister play
cards together.

Mel and her sisters like putting on shows for their parents.

This is Nina
with her mum
and her mum's
sister – Nina's
Auntie Janet.

Do you have a sister?
What's she like?

Family words

Here are some words people use when talking about their sister or family.

Names for children:
Sister, Brother; Daughter, Son.

Names for parents:
Father, Daddy, Dad, Pa;
Mother, Mummy, Mum, Ma.

Names of other relatives:
Grandchildren; Grandparents;
Grandmother, Granny, Grandma;
Grandfather, Grandad, Grandpa;
Uncle; Aunt, Auntie; Nephew; Niece.

If we put the word 'Step' in front of a relative's name, it means that we are related to them by marriage but not by birth.

If we put the word 'Half' in front of our brother or sister, it means that one of our parents is the same and the other is different.

A family tree

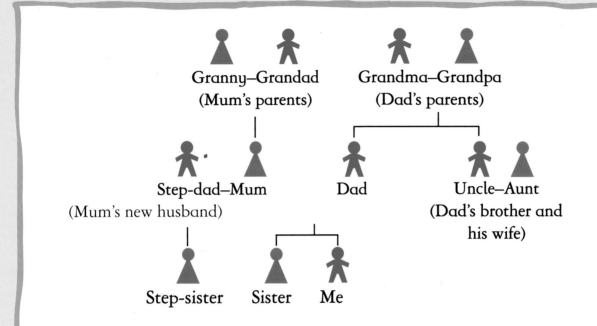

Granny–Grandad
(Mum's parents)

Grandma–Grandpa
(Dad's parents)

Step-dad–Mum
(Mum's new husband)

Dad

Uncle–Aunt
(Dad's brother and
his wife)

Step-sister   Sister   Me

You can show how you are related to all your family on a plan like this one. It is called a family tree. Every family tree is different. Try drawing your own.

Published in 2008 by Franklin Watts,
338 Euston Road, London NW1 3BH

Franklin Watts Australia
Level 17/207 Kent Street, Sydney NSW 2000

Copyright © Franklin Watts 2003

Series editor: Rachel Cooke
Art director: Jonathan Hair
Design: Andrew Crowson

A CIP catalogue record for this book
is available from the British Library.

ISBN 978 0 7496 8106 7

Printed in Hong Kong/China

Acknowledgements:
Paul Baldesare/Photofusion: 13. Bruce
Berman/Corbis: front cover main, 22. www.john-
birdsall.co.uk: front cover centre below, 2, 5. Dex
Images Inc/Corbis: 1, 14. Paul Doyle/Photofusion:
16. Jon Feingersch/ Corbis: 12. Carlos
Goldin/Corbis: front cover centre above. Sally
Greenhill, Sally & Richard Greenhill: 6, 11, 20-21.
Ronnie Kauffman/ Corbis: 8-9. Roy
McMahon/Corbis: 18. Jose Luis Pelaez/Corbis: front

cover centre top. George Shelley/Corbis: front cover
bottom. Ariel Skelley/Corbis: front cover centre.
Paula Solloway/Format: 17. Mo Wilson/Format: 19.

Whilst every attempt has been made to clear copyright should there be any inadvertent omission
please apply in the first instance to the publisher
regarding rectification.

Franklin Watts is a division of Hachette Children's
Books, an Hachette Livre UK company

Please note that some of the pictures in this book
have been posed by models.